I0476135

SHOULD MARIJUANA BE LEGALIZED IN THE UNITED STATES?

A RESEARCH PROJECT SUBMITTED TO THE FACULTY OF

NATIONAL UNIVERSITY

IN PARTIAL FULFILLMENT OF THE REQUIREMENTS FOR THE

DEGREE OF

BACHELOR OF SCIENCE IN CRIMINAL JUSTICE ADMINISTRATION

JUNE 2014

By

Fuad A Aljabri

ABSTRACT

The legalization of marijuana in the United States has been a controversial issue in recent years with those who support the legalization and those who oppose it. This paper provides a thorough research about the legalization of marijuana and its effect on the American society. The paper further provides the definition and historical development of marijuana use as well as the views of both the proponents and opponents of marijuana legalization. The focus of this study is to search for evidence that may prove the impact of marijuana use, both on the physical and psychological health of the individuals. The paper also attempts to find evidence to prove the link between marijuana and violent crime as well as the impact of legalization on the crime rate. After exploring the studies of opposing sides, the paper will evaluate the evidence to reach a conclusion about the impact of marijuana legalization on health and violent crime. Further, the paper addresses a number of theories relating to the use of marijuana such as the gateway, cognitive, and conflict theories. In addition, this paper will provide some solutions and future recommendations based on the results of the studies.

TABLE OF CONTENTS

Abstract...*i*

Table of Contents.. ii-iii

Chapter I: <u>Introduction</u>

    Background of the Study 1

    Statement of the Problem..3

    Purpose and Objectives 4

    Rationale of the Study 5

    Definition of Terms..5

    Limitations of the Study 6

    Theoretical Framework 7

    Research Hypothesis 9

    Summary of Remaining Chapters 9

Chapter II: Literature Review 10

    The Legalization of Medical Marijuana 11

    Who Supports and Opposes..16

    Marijuana and Health 17

    Marijuana and Violent Crime 19

    Marijuana as a Gateway...20

    Marijuana and Cognitive Theory 22

    Marijuana and Conflict Theory..23

Chapter III: <u>Results</u>

Marijuana is Medicine 26

Marijuana is not Medicine 30

Marijuana and Violent Crime 35

Marijuana as a Gateway..39

Evaluation 41

Chapter IV: Discussion, Conclusion, and Recommendations

Discussion 42

Conclusion 47

Recommendations...50

References..52

Copyright Page 59

Chapter I: Introduction

Background of the Study

Marijuana is one of the most common drugs in America. Simply put, marijuana is the Mexican Spanish equivalent name for cannabis. In fact, marijuana is the compound word for Mary and Juana or Mary Jane. By contrast, cannabis is considered to be the mother plant from which many types of drugs are derived, including marijuana and hashish. It is worth noting that "marijuana is found in the flowering tops and leaves of the cannabis-sativa (also known as hemp) plant. The leaves of the plant always grow in odd numbers." (Swanson, Chamelin, Territo, & Taylor, 2009, p. 646) Further, there are many slang names used by people in different regions and places to describe the cannabis plant, such as pot, grass, herb, weed, Mary Jane, reefer, skunk, boom, gangster, chronic, and ganja (Nida, 2014).

Marijuana is considered to be the oldest psychoactive plant known to humanity. The plant is "botanically classified as a member of the family Cannabaceae and the genus Cannabis" (Grinspoon & Bakalar, 1993, p. 1). The marijuana plant was first introduced to America in 1545 by the Spanish conquerors. Afterwards, specifically in 1611, the English made it as a major harvest alongside with tobacco and it was cultivated as a source of fiber

1

(Marijuana History, n.d.). It is worth mentioning that marijuana used to be legal under both federal and state laws. However, by the end of 1936, all 48 states began to enact laws to regulate marijuana. By the same token, the federal government followed the same path of regulating marijuana by enacting the Marihuana Tax Act of 1937 which imposed certain restrictions on the growing and transactions of marijuana. Due to the increased use and sale of marijuana in the mid of 1960s, Congress enacted the Comprehensive Drug Abuse prevention and Control Act of 1970 which classified marijuana as a dangerous and addictive drug by placing it in Schedule I (Merino, 2011). By contrast, some states have enacted laws to allow the growing and use of marijuana for medical reasons by physicians' prescription only. For example, "in 1996, California voters passed Proposition 215, making the Golden State the first in the union to allow for the medical use of marijuana. Since then, 19 more states, and the District of Columbia have enacted similar laws" (State Medical Marijuana Laws, 2014). Thus, the future of marijuana comprehensive legalization both at the federal and state level has not being determined yet until further research is conducted to prove that the use and sale of marijuana is safe and beneficial. Currently, there is a move in the United States toward the legalization of marijuana for medical purposes, and this move has already been witnessed in twenty two states including California. Perhaps the most important act concerning the use and abuse of marijuana in the United States was the Comprehensive Drug Abuse Prevention and Control Act enacted in 1970 which placed marijuana in the category of the most serious substances (Freda, 2010). Simply, this act had classified marijuana as "having high potential for abuse, no medical use, and not safe to use without medical supervision" (Cardinale, 2014). Since then many attempts have been made to fully legalize marijuana at both at the state and federal level, but all have failed.

Problem Statement

Although marijuana has been around since Roman times, it has recently attracted a great deal of media attention and much ink has been spilled regarding the topic of legalization. Even though many Americans approve of marijuana use and many states are moving toward the legalization of marijuana, there is very little consensus concerning the effects of cannabis on public health and safety. According to a Gallup Poll, one third of Americans favor marijuana legalization, and about a half of them believe that marijuana should remain illegal. The poll also found that while most Americans oppose the legalization, they tend to see it as a national and social

3

problem (Saieva, 2008). The problem seems to be that marijuana use is on the increase and the states are moving very quickly into legalizing it, yet they do not know enough about the possible consequences of sustained use and sale of this drug.

Purpose and Objectives of the Study

As there is very little consensus about the benefits of legalization, this paper will examine existing research and theory to explore the question of whether marijuana is detrimental or beneficial to the well-being of society and the health of the individuals who live in it. The purpose of this study is to search reliable and valid information on marijuana to determine the impact of Marijuana legalization on the American society. In addition, the study will shed light on the alleged benefits of marijuana and how it will help individuals treat their medical problems. The focus of this study is to search for evidence that may prove the impact of marijuana both on the physical and psychological health of the individuals. Further, the research will focus on the link between marijuana and violent crime as well as the impact of legalization on the crime rate. Moreover, this research study will provide some solutions and future recommendation based on the findings of the research.

Rationale of the Study

Given the importance of public safety and health, it is imperative that this study investigates the problem of marijuana legalization and how it will have an adverse impact on the health in general and crime in particular. Also, it is important that this paper examines the issue from all its angles; that is, to research and examine the issue objectively taking into our consideration the views of both sides; those who support the legalization and those who oppose it. By doing so, the research study will reach a rationale point at which it could weigh both the advantages and disadvantages of marijuana legalization. This means that the study could answer the research question: Should marijuana be legalized in the United States?

Definition of Terms

Cannabis sativa: A tall plant with a stiff upright stem, divided serrated leaves, and glandular hairs. It is used to produce hemp fiber and as a psychotropic drug.

Cannabinoid: Any of a group of closely related compounds that include cannabinol and the active constituents of cannabis.

Emphysema: A condition in which the air sacs of the lungs are damaged and enlarged, causing breathlessness.

Glaucoma: A condition of increased pressure within the eyeball, causing gradual loss of sight.

Hashish: An extract of the cannabis plant, containing concentrations of the psychoactive resins.

Hemp: The cannabis plant, especially when grown for its fiber.

Oculomotor: Of or relating to the motion of the eye.

Schizophrenia: A long-term mental disorder of a type involving a breakdown in the relation between thought, emotion, and behavior, leading to faulty perception, inappropriate actions and feelings, withdrawal from reality.

Tetrahydrocannabinol (THC): A crystalline compound that is the main active ingredient of cannabis.

Visuomotor: Relating to or denoting the coordination of movement and visual perception by the brain (Oxford Dictionaries, n.d.).

Limitations

This research study is limited to secondary data collected by different researchers at a given period of time. Further, the study is limited to the states in which the use and sale of marijuana for medical purposes have been legalized specifically the states of California, Colorado, Washington, and

Oregon. In addition, this study is limited to a certain period of time; from 1985 to 2014.

Theoretical Framework

This paper will attempt to shed light on some social theories that explain why people use marijuana and how these theories affect the process of marijuana legalization. For example, the conflict theory suggests that there is a conflict between two groups of people which results in rebellion against the norms. In fact, this theory "has been used to explain diverse human behavior, such as educational practices that either sustain or challenge the status quo, cultural customs regarding the elderly, and criminal behavior" (Millard, 2013). The conflict theory further suggests that there is a struggle between the poor and rich classes in terms of defining and making laws that solely affects the poor who are powerless to change these laws resulting in a conflict and rebellion.

Another important theory affecting the use of marijuana is the gateway theory which simply suggests that the use of marijuana is literally the entry gate to other drugs. That is, those who use marijuana, they will more likely use other illicit drugs such as heroin and cocaine. For instance, the "advocates of marijuana prohibition have long argued that marijuana use may not appear harmful to an individual, but is a marker that the individual is ultimately headed for trouble as a result of their marijuana use alone" (Marijuana Research, 1995). Other research studies suggest that there is a casual relationship between the use of marijuana and other illicit drugs. They contend that "initial experiences with cannabis, which are frequently rated as pleasurable, may encourage continued use of cannabis and also broader experimentation. They further point out that "seemingly safe early experiences with cannabis may reduce the perceived risk of, and therefore barriers to, the use of other drugs" (Lynskey et al., 2003).

In addition, this study will explain the link between the cognitive theory and marijuana use. A number of studies have found that the continuous use of marijuana adversely affects the cognitive system and cause it to decline. The researchers point out that "cannabis is known to produce substantial acute effects on human cognition and visuomotor skills. Many recent studies additionally revealed rather long-lasting effects on basic oculomotor control, especially after chronic use." (Shrivastava, Johnston, & Tsuang, 2011)

Research Hypothesis

If the use and sales of marijuana is legalized in the United States, then violent crime will increase and the physical and psychological health of marijuana users will be negatively impacted.

Summary of Remaining Chapters

In Chapter two, the paper will present the views of the opposing sides; that is, the arguments for marijuana legalization and the arguments against legalization. Secondary data will be used for this type of research. After presenting the views of both sides in Chapter two (Literature Review), the paper will analyze the findings (results) in Chapter three. Finally, Chapter four will be the forum for discussing the issue of marijuana legalization based on the results and findings of earlier research.

Chapter II: Literature Review

A considerable amount of literature has been published on cannabis specifically marijuana. These studies classify marijuana into three species: cannabis sativa, cannabis indica, and cannabis ruderalis. In fact, Cannabis sativa is the most commonly used and recognized among the other species due to its ability to produce more fiber and oil. For many years, the plant has been used for making clothes as well as lighting and soap. Nevertheless, cannabis is widely used at the present time for intoxication and medical treatments. Marijuana is usually extracted from the flowers of the female plant (Grinspoon & Bakalar, 1993). The National Institute on Drug Abuse defines marijuana as the dry parts of the hemp plant which is scientifically called Cannabis sativa. These dry parts include seeds, stems, and flowers that contain the most effective psychoactive chemical called delta-9-tetrahydrocannabinol or commonly known as THC (NIDA, 2014).

Numerous studies have attempted to explain the use of cannabis throughout history. For example, Dr. Howard E. Doweiko in his book titled *Concepts of Chemical Dependency* mentioned that the Chinese physicians have used the cannabis to treat some diseases such as malaria, constipation, child birth, and as an anesthetic for surgery. During the nineteenth century, cannabis was also used for medical purposes to treat headaches and migraine (Doweiko, 2009) However, during the early years of the twentieth century, people began to view cannabis as an abusing drug as the researchers determined its ineffectiveness as a medicinal drug. Some historians have argued that marijuana was first introduced into the American society by the Mexican immigrants during the same period. This recreation drug was soon embraced by others specifically the jazz musicians. During the Prohibition of alcohol in 1920s marijuana emerged and became more popular (Doweiko, 2009).

The Legalization Of Medical Marijuana

Many research studies have mentioned that people have used marijuana as medicine to cure certain types of diseases and medical conditions such as pain, insomnia, lack of appetite, and depression. For instance, during the period 1838-1840, William Brooke O'Shaughnessy, a surgeon and professor of chemistry at the Medical College of Calcutta, conducted a research study on patients in India regarding the medicinal effects of marijuana on some diseases, such as tetanus, rabies, and rheumatism. After returning to England, he brought the same drug with him to be popular medicine among the British people. Soon many articles were published about the medical effects of marijuana both in the European and American journals (Goode, 1999; Roffman, 1982).

It is worth noting that during the early years of the twentieth century marijuana used to be legal both at the state and federal level. Nevertheless, by the end of 1936, the states began to regulate the use and sale of marijuana. As a result, the use of marijuana for medical treatment was replaced by new invented types of modern medications such as aspirin and morphine. Similarly, the federal government followed through by enacting the Marijuana Tax Act of 1937 which imposed certain restrictions on the growing and sale of marijuana. Due to the widespread of marijuana use and sale in the mid of 1960s, the Congress enacted the Comprehensive Drug Abuse Prevention and Control Act of 1970 which placed marijuana in Schedule I (Merino, 2011). This means that this type of drug is dangerous and addictive and should not be used by individuals under all circumstances.

In recent years, there have been several attempts by the states to legalize marijuana for medical purposes contrary to the laws and regulations enacted by the Federal government. Some states have partially succeeded in their attempts and began allowing people to use and sell marijuana for medical reasons by physician's prescription only. A good example of this trend can be clearly witnessed in the states of California, Oregon, Washington, and Colorado. For example, Proposition 215 of 1996 passed in California to allow certain patients to use marijuana to treat a variety of medical conditions (Gutwillig, 2009).

The proponents of medical marijuana legalization contend that marijuana is less harmless than other drugs known to be more addictive and abusive such as cocaine and heroin. They further point out to the ample benefits of this plant to treat a wide range of illnesses such as chronic pain associated with HIV, diabetes, and trauma. For instance, in 2010, the Center for Medicinal Cannabis Research conducted a study in California to determine the positive effects of marijuana on patients suffering from chronic pain related to HIV infection and other medical cases. In their report, they proclaimed that the administration of marijuana has played an effective role in decreasing the pain for a number of patients (Merino, 2011). On the other hand, the opponents of marijuana legalization argue that marijuana is very harmful and, therefore, it should not be considered as a conventional drug to treat illnesses. For example, Mark Kraus, a physician in Connecticut, and a member of the board of directors of the American Society of Addiction

Medicine, argued that smoked marijuana is very dangerous to health because it contains toxic and cancerous elements that could affects the lungs especially of those affected with HIV and lung cancer (Merino, 2011).

Given the dangers associated with marijuana use, the opponents of the legalization of medical marijuana further contend that there are many myths about marijuana that people do not realize the consequences of using this illicit and dangerous drug. The evidence can be clearly seen in a report prepared by the Office of National Drug Control Policy in which they emphasized the health consequences of marijuana use and misuse. They reported that marijuana contains more harmful smoke of carcinogenic hydrocarbons than tobacco which plays a big role in causing cancer to the respiratory system and affecting the immune system as well. They also found that there is a high risk of lung disease associated with smoking marijuana, and the prolonged use of marijuana plays a significant role in increasing many respiratory problems such as coughing, emphysema, and bronchitis (Tardiff, 2008).

In addition, the advocates of marijuana legalization argue that the legalization would reduce the number of people convicted of possession and dealing with marijuana and, as a result, reducing the prison population of those sentenced with drug-related offenses. They further argue that those convicted of crimes related to marijuana are more likely to receive harsh and long sentences. For example, Ryan King and Marc Mauer in their report titled *"The War on Marijuana: The Transformation of the War on Drugs in the 1990"*, contend that enforcing marijuana laws is very costly to law enforcement, courts, as well as the correctional system. They argue that the high number of arrests, case processing, and housing inmates, is draining the budget and resources of the criminal justice system (Tuyl, 2007).

Nevertheless, the opponents of marijuana legalization argue that there is only a small number of people convicted of marijuana-related crimes. They contend that the high number of incarcerated persons is exclusively related to inmates in federal prisons and those convicted with other crimes linked to their marijuana use. For example, Dr. Eric Sevigny, a criminologist at the University of South Carolina, estimates that "only about 8 percent of state and federal prison inmates serving time for drug law violations were marijuana-only offenders" (Caulkins, Hawken, Kilmer & Kleiman, 2012). Further, Jonathan Caulkins, a professor of Operations and Public Policy at Carnegie Mellon University, along with co-authors of the book *"Marijuana Legalization- What Everyone Need to Know"*, argue that the legalization of marijuana would make it available and easy to obtain by many people. Moreover, legalizing marijuana would play a significant role in reducing the price of marijuana which leads to more people buying and using this drug (Caulkins, Hawken, Kilmer & Kleiman, 2012).

Who Supports And Opposes Marijuana Legalization?

The legalization of marijuana has been a controversial issue in recent years in the United States with those who support the legalization and those who oppose it. Both sides have different opinions on the issue and they cite different reasons to support their claims. In fact, several factors affect the views of people on the legalization such as age, religion, race, region, and political affiliation. For instance, younger people are more likely to support the legalization than older ones. Further, the liberals, non-religious, African-American, Whites, and Westerners are in favor of marijuana legalization even though their support varies and fluctuates over their lifespan (Caulkins, Hawken, Kilmer & Kleiman, 2012). Additional evidence suggests that the public views towards the legalization of marijuana are influenced by political affiliation and cultural perspectives. Although politics plays a significant role in shaping the opinions of the individuals, some people have mixed feelings and contradictory views about the issue of marijuana legalization regardless of their political affiliation. Furthermore, experience and demographic change would be considered important factors of whether people support or oppose marijuana legalization (Galston & Dionne, 2013).

Marijuana And Health

The positive and negative effects of marijuana on health have been a controversial issue for relatively many years and this controversy has increased recently. The arguments in favor of the marijuana use attempted to explain the medical benefits of marijuana and how it could treat a variety of illnesses and medical conditions. The proponents explained that marijuana could treat the eye pressure disease known as glaucoma by lowering the intraocular pressure of the eyes. They also argued that marijuana could treat epilepsy due to the anticonvulsant properties of cannabis that was believed to be an effective medicine to treat patients suffering from this disease (Grinspoon & Bakalar, 1993). Moreover, it has been suggested that marijuana could provide relief for many patients who suffer from migraine, lack of appetite, nausea, depression, and pain related to arthritic conditions. The advocates also suggested that marijuana may be used as an appetite stimulant especially for patients suffering from nausea associated with AIDS-related drugs (Shohov, 2003; Merino, 2011).

With that being said, the opponents of medical marijuana maintain that marijuana is dangerous and harmful drug that should not be used to treat medical problems. They argue that marijuana contains more harmful smoke of carcinogenic hydrocarbons than tobacco which plays a big role in causing cancer to the respiratory system and affecting the immune system as well. Moreover, there is a high risk of lung disease associated with smoking marijuana, and the prolonged use of marijuana plays a significant role in increasing many respiratory problems such as coughing, emphysema, and bronchitis. In addition, smoking marijuana affects both the brain and heart as it could alter the brain and cause the heart rate to double (Brick, 2008; Tardiff, 2008). Furthermore, critics point to the psychological and mental risks associated with the use of marijuana. They maintain that marijuana adversely affects the mental health of the individuals as there is a link between the use of marijuana and schizophrenia as well as other mental illnesses (Carroll, 2006; Tuyle, 2007; Gillard, 2009).

Equally important is the negative impact of marijuana on the physical health of the individuals especially those who take other drugs alongside marijuana. For instance, marijuana can affect the reproductive health by decreasing the testosterone levels and impacting the sperm quality and therefore damaging the fertility. The same holds true for women's reproduction system especially if they are heavy users of marijuana (Carroll, 2006; Gelder, Reefhius, Herron, Williams & Roeleveld, 2011). Further, marijuana is known to have a negative impact on the lungs and heart. The evidence suggests that smoked marijuana could cause a variety of ailments and disease such as lung cancer, bronchitis, lung infections, heart attack, asthma, blood pressure, and other respiratory problems (Shohov, 2003; Brick, 2008; Gillard, 2009).

Marijuana And Violent Crime

The advocates of marijuana maintain that there is no relationship between marijuana and violent crime. They contend that violent crime is closely associated with the use of other illicit drugs taken along with marijuana. They further proclaim that the link between crime and marijuana is solely attributed to its prohibition. In addition, they maintain that marijuana use is commonly related to property and drug crimes but not violent crimes (Morris, TenEyck, Barnes & Kovandzic, 2014). However, the opponents of marijuana argue that marijuana use is highly associated with violent crime. The evidence suggests that intimate partner violence during adolescent years is linked to marijuana use. Further, marijuana is found to be one of the causes of physical fighting in schools among teenagers especially if mixed with alcohol. In addition, the prolonged use of marijuana can have an adverse impact on the nervous system in a way that leads to violent behavior (Markowitz, 2000; Reingle, Staras, Jennings, Branchini & Maldonado-Molina, 2002).

It is worth mentioning that the link between violence and marijuana takes on mixed dimensions in terms of the type of the relationship. For example, marijuana is considered to be the primary cause of violence and aggression, yet in other occasions the relationship does not exist. Also, it has been suggested that the use of marijuana will negatively affect the nervous system of the users resulting in the temporary impairment of the inhibitions that control the behavior of the individuals which depends on many factors such as the condition of the individual and whether he or she has used other drugs (Abel, 1977).

Marijuana As A Gateway

The gateway theory is commonly associated with marijuana. The theory suggests that the use of marijuana is literally the entry gate to other drugs. It means that those who use marijuana will more likely use other illegal drugs such as cocaine and heroin. For example, the opponents of marijuana legalization contend that mere use of marijuana may not seem a bad thing, but consequently will lead to many troubles along the way (Marijuana Research, 1995). Also, the evidence suggests that when the individuals experience some of the temporary pleasant feelings associated with the use of marijuana, they will more likely try to experiment other drugs. In addition, the casual relationship is an important factor affecting the gateway theory. This means that those who use marijuana will be more vulnerable to many challenges that lead them to try other drugs, and therefore increase their social contact with addicted and experienced peers (Lynskey et al., 2003; Caulkins, Hawken, Kilmer & Kleiman, 2012).

Furthermore, the White House Office of National Drug Control Policy maintains that adults, who have been using marijuana during their adolescent age, have become regular users of heroin and cocaine. In fact, the problem lies with the perception and attitudes of the individuals about marijuana. Those who view the use of marijuana as enjoyable experience will more likely overcome the fears associated with the use of drugs in general (Tuyl, 2007; Gillard, 2009). This explains the theory of gateway and its direct connection to marijuana use.

Marijuana And Cognitive Theory

The prolonged use of marijuana adversely affects the cognitive system and causes it to decline. The impairment increases with the number of doses and the amount of time as well as other factors. In fact, the chemicals found in the marijuana primarily the THC play a significant role in the process of harming the brain and its cognitive parts. Furthermore, the heavy use of marijuana can have a negative impact on motor skills, perceptions, and judgment, which in turn affects driving skills. This is due to the lack of coordination and loss of short memory associated with distorted perceptions and diminished judgment (Tuyl, 2007). Moreover, the continued use of marijuana is believed to have a negative impact on both the long-term and short-term memory (Shrivastava, Johnston, & Tsuang, 2011; Nunley, Alexander, Corns, Geer, 2000) In addition, the constant and heavy use of marijuana can adversely affect the learning development especially when the initiation of marijuana begins at an early age. Consequently, this leads to permanent damage to the cognitive system that cannot be restored even after the users stop using marijuana (NIDA, 2014).

Marijuana And Conflict Theory

The conflict theory suggests that there is a conflict between two groups of people which results in rebellion against the norms. In fact, this theory explains the "diverse human behavior, such as educational practices that either sustain or challenge the status quo, cultural customs regarding the elderly, and criminal behavior" (Millard, 2013). Furthermore, the theory suggests that many conflicting factors have contributed to the problem of drug use including marijuana. For example, the economic developments have played an important role in the social conflict between the poor and the powerful. This means that the living conditions of the poor are negatively impacted as they lose the political power to change their status quo. As a result, the drug dealers will more likely take advantage of the situation to become an attractive alternative for jobs (Goode, 2008). In addition, the conflict theory suggests that the rich and powerful attempt to exploit the legalization by producing more marijuana in order to tax the poor. This will create social and economic conflict between small and big businesses, which results in fewer jobs for the poor (Haans, 1994).

The following chapter will explore a number of important research studies and their results in further detail. Also, it will provide some statistical analysis and evaluations about the impact of marijuana use on health and violent crime. Further, data tables and figures will be provided to show the results in their actual values.

Chapter III: Results

Introduction

This Chapter evaluates the results as well as the discussions from the field study. In addition, the Chapter is seeking to examine the impacts of legalizing marijuana on the American people. Similarly, the study seeks to evaluate the alleged medical benefits of marijuana to treat some diseases. On the other hand, the study focuses and attempts to analyze the relationship between marijuana and crime as well as how the legalization of marijuana influences the rate of crime (Borini, 2004). The data used was obtained from secondary sources.

Hypothesis: The hypothesis is as follows: If the use and sale of marijuana is legalized in the United States, then violent crime will increase and the physical and psychological health of marijuana users will be negatively impacted. This section will focus on the studies that support and oppose the legalization of marijuana.

Marijuana Is Medicine

Study # 1

According to Lester Grinspoon (Harvard Medical School) and James

Bakalar (Harvard Mental Health Letter), there are three species of marijuana;

Cannabis indica, Cannabis ruderalis and Cannabis sativa. Based on the data

obtained from the field, Cannabis sativa is mostly recognized and used

compared to other species because they produce abundant oil and fiber

(Grinspoon & Bakalar, 1993). The figure below shows the three types of

Cannabis sativa and their extent of usage:

Figure # 1: Types of Marijuana Species

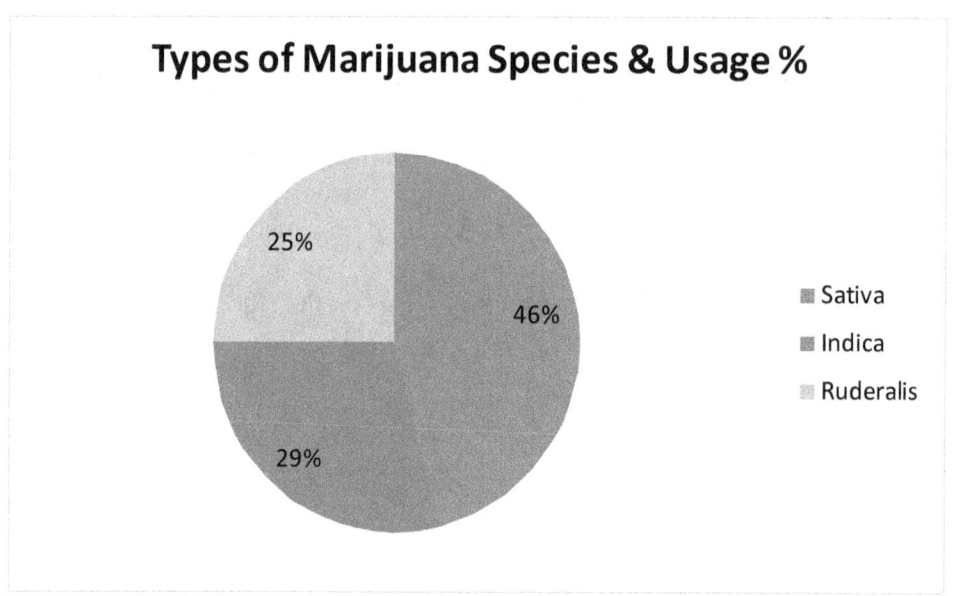

Note. Adapted from *Marijuana, the forbidden medicine*, by Grinspoon &
Bakalr, 1993, New Haven: Yale University press.

The figure above illustrates how Cannabis sativa is widely used than the other species, 46% of the people using marijuana opt to use sativa, and 29% preferred indica, and only a few people opted for Cannabis ruderalis (Carnot, 2011).

The results based on the research studies enhance the understanding of the use of marijuana and its legalization. The scientific literature has shown that many people have been abusing marijuana under the pretext of medical purposes. They have had a strong perception that marijuana is used for medication, but in fact it is being used for leisure and recreation. The results indicate that 56% of most youth have used marijuana; some of them end up using it without knowing that they were using an illegal and dangerous drug. Nowadays, youth are drawn into using the drug, for example added as food spices (Gfroerer, 2002).

The scholarly research directed by Grinspoon and Bakalar confirmed the use of marijuana as medicine, and showed that marijuana could heal various ailments and diseases. The finding was illustrated by a scientific research prepared by the University of Iowa. The researchers used random samples by giving oral THC or placebo to cancer patients who were suffering from critical pain. The medication was given in doses between 5 to 10 mg, and sometimes they increased the dose to 20 mg. The study showed that the pain was relieved for a number of hours depending on the doses of the THC. The result of this study established that THC was a pain killer and had soothing effects especially when given in large doses. Also, THC was proven to have only a few physical reactions. The researchers gave oral doses of THC to hospitalized cancer patients to relieve the severe pain they were suffering (Grinspoon & Bakalar, 1993).

Study # 2.

The Center for Medicinal Cannabis Research (CMCR) was founded in the University of California at San Diego School of Medicine. The CMCR has conducted many therapeutic research studies to prove the medical benefits of marijuana for patients who are struggling with HIV/AIDS, cancer, seizures, glaucoma and migraine. According to their Journal of Neurology, Dr. Daniel Abrams et al prepared their study to establish the impact of smoked marijuana on the nervous system and the pain suffered by the HIV-infected patients. The outcome of this study established that the pain was reduced by 34% even if the subjects were given only low-grade cannabis (Merino, 2011). Other medical studies were conducted to prove the medical benefits of marijuana, such as the study prepared by the Center for Medicinal Cannabis Research in California in 2010. The purpose of this study was to determine the positive effects of marijuana on patients suffering from chronic pain related to HIV infection and other medical cases. In their report, they proclaimed that the administration of marijuana had played an effective role in decreasing the pain for a number of patients (Merino, 2011).

It is worth noting that the above-mentioned findings may explain the reason beyond the thrust for the legalization of marijuana for medical purposes. It also explains why some states have passed legislation to legalize medical marijuana. The chart below is a good example to illustrate the number of patients who can legally have an access to medical marijuana:

Figure 2. Medical Marijuana Patients by State

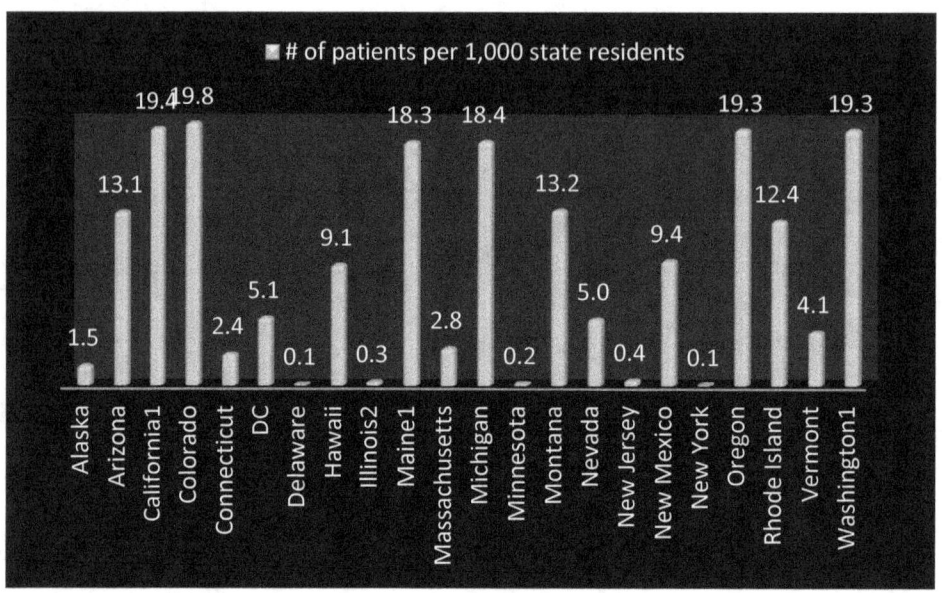

Note. Adapted from *How Many People in the United States Use Medical Marijuana,* by ProCon.org, 2012. US Census Bureau's 2011 data.

The chart above illustrates all the States where the patients are legally allowed to use medical marijuana. California is at the top of all these states.

Marijuana Is Not Medicine

Study # 1.

A recent research study prepared by the Office of National Drug Control Policy was a good example that explains the health consequences of using marijuana. The study found that marijuana contains more harmful smoke of carcinogenic hydrocarbons than tobacco which plays a big role in causing cancer to the respiratory system and affecting the immune system as

30

well. The research also found that there is a high risk of lung disease associated with smoking marijuana, and the prolonged use of marijuana plays a significant role in increasing many respiratory problems such as coughing, emphysema, and bronchitis. Furthermore, the study mentions the number of emergency room visits by marijuana users and how it increased 167 percent since 1994. They further added that in 2001, there were more than 11,000 emergency room visits by marijuana users. In addition, the research have revealed that smoking marijuana affects both the brain and heart as it could alter the brain and cause the heart rate to double (Tardiff, 2008).

The figure below shows the negative effects of marijuana on the health of the users:

Figure 3. The Negative Effects of Marijuana on Health

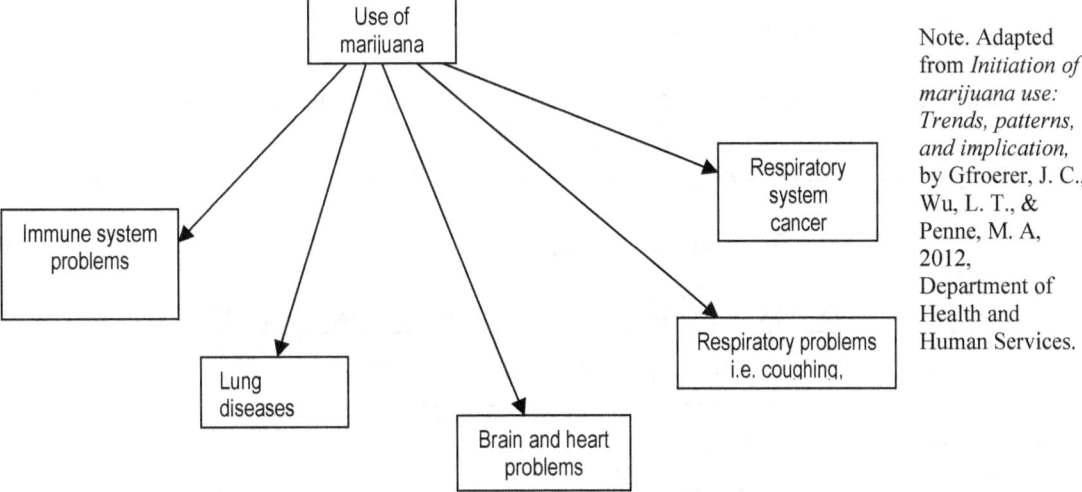

Note. Adapted from *Initiation of marijuana use: Trends, patterns, and implication,* by Gfroerer, J. C., Wu, L. T., & Penne, M. A, 2012, Department of Health and Human Services.

The above chart clearly shows various negative effects of on the health and well-being of the users. Examples of these effects are brain disorder and heart problems, immune system problems, lung diseases, and respiratory cancer.

Study # 2.

Furthermore, several researchers have found that marijuana is linked to psychological and mental health problems. An example of that was a major study conducted by a distinguished group of doctors and professors from Stony Brook University in New York: Daniel Foti, Roman Kotov, Lin Guey & Evelyn Bromet. Their study was based on the assessment of 229 patients suffering from schizophrenia over the course of ten years. The researchers concluded that the rate of the lifetime users of marijuana was 66.2 percent. Besides, they found that this particular use was linked to earlier mental disorder. In their study, the researchers used different controls and variables to measure the results such as other drug use, social and economic status, antipsychotic medications, gender, age, and other signs (Foti, Kotov, Guey & Bromet, 2010). The following tables show the study:

Table 1: Associations of Demographic Characteristics with Past-month Cannabis Use

Variable	Full Sample		Cannabis Users at		Cannabis Nonusers		Comparison
	N=	229	Base-line (N=	23	Base-line (N=	202	

	N	%	N	%	N	%	Odds Ratio	95% CI
Gender								
Male	149	65.10%	18	78.30%	128	63.40%	2.08	.74-5.84
Female	80	34.90%	5	21.70%	74	36.60%		
Socioeconomic status of family of origin								
Low (semiskilled or unskilled)	81	35.4	7	30.4	74	36.6		
Medium (skilled)	83	36.2	12	52.2	69	34.2		
High (white collar)	65	28.4	4	17.4	59	29.2		
Lifetime cannabis use (prior to baseline	149	66.2	23	100	123	61.8		
	MEAN	SD	MEAN	SD	MEAN	SD	t	
Age at baseline	28.02	8.55	23.65	6.37	28.47	8.69	2.58	223
Age at onset of psychosis	25.6	7.76	22.61	6.21	25.99	7.91	1.98	212

Note. Adapted from *Cannabis use and the course of schizophrenia: 10-year follow-up after first hospitalization*, by Foti, D. J., Kotov, R., Guey, L. T., & Bromet, E. J., 2010, American Journal of Psychiatry, 167(8), 987-993

Table 2. Assessment Point

Measure	Assessment Point									
	Base line	N= 225	Month 6	N=184	Year2	N =166	Year 4	N =143	Year 10	N =162
	N	%	N	%	N	%	N	%	N	%
Prevalence										
Users	23	10.20%	26	14.10%	30	18.10%	19	13.30%	16	9.90%
Nonusers	202	89.80%	158	85.90%	136	81.90%	124	86.70%	146	90.10%

Note. Adapted from *Cannabis use and the course of schizophrenia: 10-year follow-up after first hospitalization*, by Foti, D. J., Kotov, R., Guey, L. T., & Bromet, E. J., 2010, American Journal of Psychiatry, 167(8), 987-993

The above tables clearly show the correlated and direct relationship between the use of marijuana and the illness of schizophrenia (Foti, Kotov, Guey & Bromet, 2010).

Study # 3.

Another important study of marijuana use and its physical impact on health is conducted by a team of researchers who measured the relationship between marijuana use and mortality. The authors Sidney Sorrin, Joseph Beck, Irene Tekawa, Charles Quesenberry & Gary Friedman (Kaiser Permanente Medical Care Program Research Division) conducted their study on different segments of the society such as age, gender, marital status, educational level, as well as AIDS and non-AIDS population. The authors found that the use of marijuana was not linked to the increased risk of mortality for men who were not infected with AIDS. The relative risk was only 1.12, and the confidence interval was 0.89 compared to women. Regarding the AIDS patients, they found that marijuana was highly linked to the increased risk of mortality in men with AIDS. The relative risk was 1.90 or 95 percent, and the confidence control was 1.33 or 2.73 percent. The authors interpreted the surprising results to a third variable that they could not control which was the behavior of homosexual men. They attributed this analysis to the AIDS database maintained by Kaiser Permanente (Sidney, Beck, Tekawa, Quesenberry &

Friedman, 1997).

Marijuana And Violent Crime

Study # 1.

Some research studies argue that medical marijuana is not linked to

violent crime. An example of these studies was a research conducted by a

team in University of Texas at Dallas. The researchers Robert Morris, Michael

TenEyck, John (JC) Barnes, and Tomislav Kovendzic obtained their

information from the State of Texas data as the main source of their research.

The authors concluded that there is no relationship between marijuana

legalization and violent crime when measured individually. The authors found

that the crime rate from 1990 to 2006 dropped in the states that passed the

legislation to legalize medical marijuana. They further found that the violent

crimes of aggravated assault, robbery, and homicide were reduced in these

states. However, the authors admitted that there was an exception to their

finding which was the violent crime of forcible rape. The authors further

found that the effect of the marijuana legalization was only significant in

certain crimes specifically assault and homicide. According to the table, they

found 24 percent reduction in the crimes of homicide and assault for every year after the passage of the law. The authors also did not find any increase in the crimes of burglary and robbery. They concluded that the legalization of marijuana did not have an effect on any crime. Nevertheless, the authors admitted that the results were inconsistent because they did not include other variables and factors in their analysis, which if controlled for, they will have a significant impact on their findings (Morris, TenEyck, Barnes & Kovandzic, 2014). The following table illustrates the findings:

Table 3. The Effects of Medical Marijuana Laws on Crime

The Effect of Medical Marijuana Laws on Crime:
Evidence from State Panel Data, 1990-2006

Variable	Homicide	Rape	Robbery	Assault	Burglary	Larceny	Auto Theft
Medical Marijuana Law (MML)	-0.024	-0.005	-0.016	-0.024	-0.004	-0.002	0.026
	-0.007	-0.009	-0.010	-0.013	-0.007	-0.004	-0.016
Unemployment rate	0.031	-0.001	0.039	-0.021	0.022	0.005	0.036
	-0.012	-0.014	-0.014	-0.022	-0.011	-0.009	-0.014
Employment rate	1.325	3.672	3.637	4.249	0.420	-0.584	-0.069
	-1.277	-1.156	-1.536	-1.383	-0.943	-0.747	-1.715
Poverty rate	-0.008	0.006	0.001	0.001	-0.004	-0.002	-0.007
	-0.003	-0.004	-0.005	-0.005	-0.003	-0.002	-0.004
Per-capita income	-0.013	-0.226	-0.148	-0.173	-0.194	-0.099	-0.137
	-0.057	-0.067	-0.072	-0.100	-0.048	-0.036	-0.102
Proportion aged 15 to 24	3.528	-	-3.591	-3.245	0.676	-0.266	5.279

		0.279					
	-2.447	-1.681	-3.371	-3.245	0.676	-0.266	5.279
Proportion aged 25 to 34	-4.250	-0.202	-3.478	-7.492	5.150	2.729	11.35
	-1.884	-2.038	-2.920	-3.112	-1.904	-1.712	-2.609
Proportion aged 35 to 44	-1.393	-3.083	-4.008	-13.78	-1.940	0.193	-3.558
	-2.041	-2.319	-3.366	-4.654	-1.928	-1.489	-4.075
Beer consumption	0.903	0.504	1.261	0.436	0.857	0.762	1.376
	-0.399	-0.283	-0.442	-0.576	-0.291	-0.280	-0.580
Percent college degree	-0.004	0.016	-0.032	-0.012	-0.001	0.005	-0.018
	-0.011	-0.010	-0.012	-0.017	-0.007	-0.007	-0.013
Percent metropolitan	0.015	0.022	0.004	0.004	-0.006	-0.005	0.009
	-0.007	-0.008	-0.009	-0.015	-0.008	-0.006	-0.014
Prisoners per 100k	-45.68	-20.41	-33.92	41.979	-7.186	9.724	-56.41
	-33.96	-22.44	-35.01	-30.05	-26.13	-18.58	-48.73
Police officers per 100k	-0.001	0.000	-0.002	-0.001	0.000	0.001	-0.001
	-0.001	-0.001	-0.001	-0.001	-0.001	-0.001	-0.002
R^2	0.500	0.460	0.580	0.440	0.830	0.750	0.440

Note. Adapted from The Effects of Medical Marijuana laws on Crime, by Morris, TenEyck, Barnes & Kovandzic, 2014, PloS one, 9(3), e92816.

Study # 2.

In another longitudinal study, Dr. Jennifer Reingle (University of Florida, College of Medicine) and her associates Stephanie Staras, Wesley Jennings, Jennifer Branchini, and Mildred Maldonado-Molina (University of

Florida) conducted a survey study on a group of teens and young adults whose ages were 15 to 26 years to examine the connection between intimate partner violence and marijuana use. The authors obtained the data from 9,421 teens between the years 1995 and 2008. Those who participated in the survey were both users and non-users of marijuana. They divided the group into three categories in terms of victimization, perpetration, or both. They used multinomial regression to measure the results. The authors found that the steady use of marijuana during the teen years was highly linked to partner violence during early adulthood. The regression was (2.08, P < .001) (Reingle, Staras, Jennings, Branchini & Maldonando-Molina, 2002). The table below shows the results:

Table 4. Marijuana Use (Ages 15-21) Patterns as Predictors of Intimate Partner Violence

Marijuana Use (Ages 15–21) Patterns as Predictors of Intimate Partner Violence (Age 26)

	Victim Only		Perpetrator Only		Victim and Perpetrator	
	OR	95% CI	*OR*	95% CI	*OR*	95% CI
Unadjusted model						
No marijuana use	1	—	1	—	1	—
Desisted from marijuana use	0.99	[0.78, 1.24]	1.27	[0.93, 1.75]	1.27	[1.05, 1.54]
Initiated marijuana use	1.14	[0.86, 1.50]	1.28	[0.80, 2.06]	1.54	[1.12, 2.11]
Consistent marijuana use	1.28	[0.98, 1.69]	1.84	[1.18, 2.86]	2.36	[1.89, 2.94]
Adjusted model						
No marijuana use	1	—	1	—	1	—
Desisted from marijuana use	1.1	[0.80, 1.52]	1.33	[0.83, 2.14]	1.37	[0.96, 1.96]
Initiated marijuana use	1.99	[0.78, 1.26]	1.4	[0.95, 2.05]	1.39	[1.12, 1.73]
Consistent marijuana use	1.24	[0.89, 1.73]	1.85	[1.04, 3.28]	2.08	[1.53, 2.85]
Covariates						
Peer alcohol use	0.97	[0.77, 1.18]	1.13	[0.82, 1.55]	1.24	[0.97, 1.59]
Peer marijuana use	0.92	[0.72, 1.18]	1.42	[0.97, 2.09]	1.22	[0.97, 1.54]
Parental involvement	0.98	[0.95, 1.01]	1.01	[0.96, 1.05]	0.98	[0.95, 1.02]
Parental alcohol use	0.94	[0.79, 1.11]	0.98	[0.70, 1.39]	0.74	[0.59, 0.92]
Depression	1.08	[0.90, 1.31]	1.26	[0.90, 1.76]	1.3	[1.05, 1.60]
Binge drinking	1.31	[1.03, 1.67]	0.75	[0.53, 1.09]	1.09	[0.84, 1.40]

Note. Adapted from Marijuana Use (Ages 15-21) Patterns as Predictors of Intimate Partner Violence, by Reingle et al., 2002, Journal of interpersonal violence, 27(8), 1562-1578.

Marijuana As A Gateway

Study # 1. Many research studies have attempted to prove that marijuana is the gateway to other illegal drugs. For example, Dr. Rashi Shukla (University of Central Oklahoma) conducted a research study on a group of fifty-one former and current users of marijuana between 2000 and 2002. The participants were asked to evaluate their perception of marijuana as a gateway. After conducting qualitative conversations with the participants, the author found the following: Forty-one of the participants indicated that they used alcohol and tobacco before experiencing marijuana; fifteen of them stated that they used other illegal drugs before marijuana; twenty-three of them had mixed answers; eighteen participants did not believe that marijuana was a gateway; and only ten of them supported this theory (Shukla, 2013).

Study # 2. Another study directed by Wayne Hall and Michael Lynsky (University of Queensland – Institute for Molecular Bioscience) examines the connection between the theory of gateway and marijuana. After conducting their research on both humans and animals, the authors found several relationships that explain this theory. For example, they found that the use of other illegal drugs followed the use of marijuana. They also found that early and consistent use of marijuana played an important role in determining this relationship. Furthermore, they found that other factors had played a role in the decision of marijuana users to try other drugs, such as peer pressure and association, the traits of the users, and the chemical characteristics of marijuana and their effect on the brain (Hall & Lynsky, 2005).

Evaluation

After evaluating the studies and their results about the effects of marijuana on
health and violent crime, it appeared that the results support the hypothesis
about the negative effects of marijuana and its legalization on the physical and
psychological health of the users. However, the relationship between
marijuana and violent crime is only partially supported. There are many
uncontrolled variables and factors that impact the research studies of
marijuana. As a result, further objective studies need to be conducted on this
controversial issue.

Chapter IV

Discussion, Conclusions, and Recommendations

Discussion

As previously mentioned, marijuana has a negative impact on the society in terms of crime and the well-being of individuals both physically and psychologically. Some research studies have established that there was a correlation between the use of marijuana and violent crime. Further studies have proven marijuana as dangerous and addictive drug that affects both the body and brain of the user, and as a result tragic consequences will follow. After evaluating the findings, it has become evident that the legalization of marijuana will have a negative impact on the users' health as well as criminal behavior. In fact, marijuana has proven to be a poisonous and addictive drug that can destroy both the physical and psychological health of the individuals especially those who constantly use it at an early age. Furthermore, the legalization will be a contributing factor in property and drug crimes as well as in violence.

Needless to say, the legalization of marijuana in the United States has been a controversial issue for relatively many years, and the debate has recently intensified due to the widespread of marijuana use and sale for medical purposes. The advocates of the legalization of marijuana argue that

marijuana is harmless and would not pose any health risk to the health and

well-being of human beings. They argue that there is no scientific evidence to

prove that marijuana is addictive and dangerous drug. For example, they

confirmed that the THC found in marijuana was an effective pain killer that

could relieve the severe pain suffered by cancer patients (Grinspoon &

Bakalar, 1993). It goes without saying that most of the drugs including

marijuana are pain killers. This means that they could kill the nerves and

senses that transfer the feeling of pain into the brain. Is this an effective and

appropriate method to heal and treat diseases? Is killing and numbing the

nerves a healthy way to cure the pain? For example, heroin, which is an illicit

drug, can kill and relieve the pain as well. Can we legalize heroin to treat

certain diseases and ailments? The answer is no. Drugs that numb the nerves

and alter the brain should not be used as medicine to treat and cure diseases.

They also argue that marijuana has some medical benefits for patients who are

struggling with HIV/AIDS, cancer, seizures, glaucoma, and migraine. For

example, the Center for Medicinal Cannabis research of UCSD established the

impact of smoked marijuana on the nervous system by reducing the chronic

pain for a number of HIV patients (Merino, 2011). In fact, the researchers have failed to prove that marijuana was an effective medicine to treat and heal the above-mentioned diseases. The only thing that they established was that marijuana was a pain killer. If marijuana can treat and cure serious diseases such as AIDS and cancer, it would be considered as an amazing medicine that deserves to be legalized. However, the pain killing element is nothing but a temporary relief from pain that also could be obtained by administering other drugs such as morphine, codeine, valium, and other anesthetic drugs.

In addition, the Federal government has placed marijuana in Schedule I, which means that this drug is dangerous, addictive, and should never be used as medicine to treat diseases. Yet, twenty-two states including the states of California, Colorado, Oregon, and Washington have recently legalized marijuana to be used as medicine to treat certain illnesses. This is a legal paradox that indicates a clear contradiction between the laws of the states and those of the federal government. Besides, the classification of marijuana as the most dangerous and abusive drug was not created out of nothing. There must be extensive studies and experiments conducted by the federal government before the enactment of law.

It seems that the most serious criticism of marijuana is its impact on the physical health of users especially the respiratory system. According to the

Office of National Drug Control Policy, marijuana was found to contain more harmful smoke of carcinogenic hydrocarbons than tobacco which poses a high risk of lung diseases, respiratory cancer, immune system problems, heart disease, and other serious illnesses. The study also mentioned that emergency rooms visits by marijuana users have increased 167 percent since 1994, and there were 11,000 emergency visits in 2001. The most obvious finding to emerge from this study is that marijuana is more dangerous than tobacco and other drugs in terms of its negative impact on the health of individuals. These findings suggest that marijuana must be stopped and prohibited to be used as medicine (Tardiff, 2008).

In addition to its impact on the physical health, marijuana can negatively affect the mental and psychological health of its users. The doctors found a strong link between the use of marijuana and schizophrenia. The results of their study show the negative effects of marijuana on the brain and the high potential risk associated with its constant use (Foti et al., 2010). Taken together, the findings suggest that drugs that alter the brain and cause mental problems should be avoided and never be used as medicine.

Regarding the second part of the research hypothesis, the link between marijuana and violent crime is partially supported by the previous findings.

For example, the researchers found that the crime rate from 1990 to 2006 dropped in the states that legalized medical marijuana specifically the crimes of homicide and assault. They also found a reduction in the crimes of aggravated assault and robbery. Moreover, forcible rape was excluded from the list of violent crimes (Morris et al., 2014). However, the researchers did not take into their consideration the other variables and controls when they conducted their study. If other variables are accurately measured, they will have a significant impact on the results as the authors have admitted. On the other hand, a team of doctors from the University of Florida conducted a survey study on a group of teens to determine the link between marijuana use and intimate partner violence. The authors found that the constant use of marijuana during the teen years was highly linked to partner violence during early adulthood (Reingle et al., 2002). The regression analysis indicates that there is a link between marijuana use and violent behavior. However, this use must be constant and must be taken during the adolescent years to have an effect on the early adulthood years. With that being said, the study partially supports the connection between marijuana and violent behavior.

In addition, it is very likely that those who use marijuana will attempt to use other illicit drugs. For example, socializing with peers who are using other drugs will most likely lure individual to try them either out of curiosity or by peer pressure. Besides, the personalities of individuals play a role in whether or not they will fall into this habit. In addition, the chemical properties of marijuana itself play an important role in altering the brain of users and turning them into addicts willing to try anything in order to get satisfied. As a result, marijuana should not be made legal and available for all to use because it is the gateway to other illegal drugs.

Conclusions

After evaluating both sides of the arguments, the most noticeable outcome to arise from this study is that the use of marijuana as medicine is yet to be established. That is to say, thorough and an independent research needs to be conducted on marijuana to provide convincing evidence to the public that marijuana is harmless and will not pose any health risk to human beings. After analyzing the studies, it appeared that the findings support the hypothesis about the negative impact of marijuana and its legalization on the physical and psychological health of individuals. As stated above, marijuana can negatively affect and destroy the health and lives of those who use is either for medical or recreational purposes. Due to the harmful carcinogenic hydrocarbons found in marijuana, smoked marijuana can affect the respiratory system, and it can cause lung cancer and other serious diseases as well. Besides, the constant use of marijuana plays a significant role in increasing and worsening many health conditions such as coughing, bronchitis, asthma, and the immune system. Further, marijuana is found to have serious impact on AIDS patients as it can negatively affect their mortality rate. This translates to shorter lives for AIDS patients who use marijuana as medicine to treat their conditions.

Nevertheless, the link between marijuana and violent crime is only partially supported. In fact, some studies have confirmed that there was a link between the use of marijuana and certain crimes, yet they did not find strong and convincing evidence about violent crimes. As mentioned above, many factors are yet to be taken into consideration when measuring this relationship. Without a doubt, the legalization of marijuana will have an impact on the crime rate specially property and drug crimes. When marijuana becomes legal and available, many individuals, especially young persons, tend to use it more often and as a result they become addicted to it. When the addiction occurs, the users will become so attached to the habit that they cannot abandon it under all circumstances. If they do not have sufficient money to purchase the drug, they will adopt different illegal means to obtain it such as theft, burglary, robbery, selling other illegal drugs, and joining gangs. Furthermore, those who are addicted to marijuana are more likely to adhere to violence to support their habit especially if they do not have the opportunity to commit other non-violent crimes. For example, they may commit robbery, aggravated assault, homicide, and other violent crimes to obtain either the money or the drug itself. In addition, marijuana users whose psychological health is negatively affected by the constant use of marijuana are more likely to commit sexual crimes such as rape, sexual assault, and intimate partner violence especially those who are infected with schizophrenia and other mental diseases.

Additionally, the legalization of marijuana will normalize both the use and sale of marijuana leading the society to look at this drug as normal and harmless. This will result in increasing sale and marketing of marijuana by drug cartels who exploit all the circumstances for their own benefits. For example, criminal gangs can exploit teens and young adults to sell marijuana and other illicit drugs. Needless to say, drug transactions play a big role in criminal activity among gang members and their associates. This illegal activity will have an impact on the crime rate as well as the quality of life of the individuals.

Moreover, a number of important limitations need to be taken into consideration when evaluating the study. First, the study is limited to a certain period of time; second, the study is limited to the U.S. population only specifically the states that legalized medical marijuana; third, the research is limited to secondary data, which means that it lacks direct examination and observation of the dependent and independent variables. Furthermore, the small size of the samples plays a significant role in determining the outcome of the research studies.

Needless to say, this study enhances the readers' knowledge and understanding of marijuana in general, and its impact on the physical and psychological health in particular. Also, the results add significantly to the readers' understanding of the link between marijuana use and crime. Besides, this study provides an educational and instructive body of literature about marijuana both for users and non-users.

Recommendations

Finally, it is highly recommended that further research be conducted on the legalization of marijuana and its impact on the American society. Also, future experiments need to consider all the factors and uncontrolled variables to obtain accurate and correct findings that the scientific community can rely on in their evaluations. Further, it is recommended that the states temporarily abolish the legalization of marijuana pending further research about this issue. In addition, cross-national study is required to determine the link between the use and sale of marijuana and violent crime. In addition, it is recommended that the scientific community conduct global studies on the legalization of marijuana and its social impact on the societies who have been experiencing the issue for relatively a few years. It seems that the future of marijuana legalization depends on the peoples' political and ideological views about drugs in general and medical marijuana in particular.

REFERENCES

Abel, E. L. (1977). *The relationship between cannabis and violence: A review*. Psychological Bulletin, 84(2), 193.

Adler, F., Mueller, G. O., & Laufer, W. S. (2010). *Criminology*. New York: McGraw-Hill.

Borini, P. (2004). *Possible hepatotoxicity of chronic marijuana usage*. (Sao Paulo Medical Journal.

Brick, J. (2008). *Handbook of the medical consequences of alcohol and drug abuse*. New York: Haworth Press.

Cardinale, A. (2014). *A Brief History of How Marijuana Became Illegal in the U.S. - PolicyMic*. Retrieved May 14, 2014, from http://www.policymic.com/articles/78685/a-brief-history-of-how-marijuana-became-illegal-in-the-u-s

Carnot, T. (2011). *The Impacts of Drinking Alcohol, Using Marijuana, and Smoking Cigarettes as a Teenager on the Educational Attainment and the Income of Young Adults* (Doctoral dissertation, Clemson University).Carroll, J. (2006). Marijuana: Opposing viewpoints. Detroit, MI: Greenhaven Press.

Carroll, J. (2005). *Who Supports Marijuana Legalization?* Retrieved May 15,

2014, from http://www.gallup.com/poll/19561/Who-Supports-

Marijuana-Legalization.aspx

Carroll, J. (2006). *Marijuana: Opposing viewpoints*. Detroit, MI: Greenhaven

Press.

Caulkins, J. P., Hawken, A., Kilmer, B., & Kleiman, M. (2012). *Marijuana*

legalization: What everyone needs to know.

Doweiko, H. (2009). *Concepts of Chemical Dependency* (7th ed.). Belmont,

CA: Cengage Learning.

Foti, D. J., Kotov, R., Guey, L. T., & Bromet, E. J. (2010). Cannabis use and

the course of schizophrenia: 10-year follow-up after first

hospitalization. American Journal of Psychiatry, 167(8), 987-993.

Galston, W. A., & Dionne, E. J. (2013). The New Politics of Marijuana

Legalization: Why Opinion is Changing | Brookings Institution.

Retrieved May 31, 2014, from

http://www.brookings.edu/research/papers/2013/05/29-politics-

marijuana-legalization-galston-dionne

Gelder, M. M., Reefhuis, J., Herron, A. M., Williams, M. L., & Roeleveld, N.

(2011). Reproductive health characteristics of marijuana and cocaine users: Results from the 2002 National Survey of Family Growth.

Perspectives on sexual and reproductive health, 43(3), 164-172.

Gfroerer, J. C., Wu, L. T., & Penne, M. A. (2002). Initiation of marijuana use:

Trends, patterns, and implications. Department of Health and Human

Services, Substance Abuse and Mental Health Services Administration,

Office of Applied Studies.

Gillard, A. (2009). *Marijuana.* Detroit: Greenhaven Press.

Goode, E. (1999). *Drugs in American society*. Boston: McGraw-Hill College.

Goode, E. (2008). *Drugs in American society*. Boston: McGraw-Hill Higher

Education.

Grinspoon, L., & Bakalar, J. B. (1993*). Marihuana, the forbidden medicine*.

New Haven: Yale University Press.

Gutwillig, S. (2009). *Medical marijuana in California: a history*. Los Angeles

Times [Los Angeles]. Retrieved May 30, 2014, from

http://www.latimes.com/health/la-oew-gutwillig-imler6-2009mar06-

story.html#page=1

Haans, D. (1994). *Why is There a 'War on Drugs'?* Retrieved May 31, 2014,

from http://www.druglibrary.org/schaffer/Misc/haans1.htm

Hall, W. D., & Lynskey, M. (2005). Is cannabis a gateway drug? Testing

    hypotheses about the relationship between cannabis use and the use of

    other illicit drugs. Drug and alcohol review, 24(1), 39-48.

HUMBOLDT JOURNAL OF SOCIAL RELATIONS, (35). Retrieved May

    15, 2014, from

    http://www.humboldt.edu/hjsr/docs/fwhjsrparagraph/Issue%2035%20

    First%20Article%20Shukla.pdf

Lynskey, M. T., Heath, A. C., Bucholz, K. K., Slutske, W. S., Madden, P. A.,

    Nelson, E. C., ... & Martin, N. G. (2003). *Escalation of drug use in*

    early-onset cannabis users vs co-twin controls. Jama, 289(4), 427-433.

Marijuana History. (n.d.). Retrieved May 15, 2014, from

    http://www.narconon.org/drug-information/marijuana-history.html

Marijuana Research: *The Gateway Theory -- Marijuana Use and Other Drug*

    Use. (1995). Retrieved on May 30, 2014, from

    http://www.drugscience.org/Petition/C6C.html

Merino, N. (2008). *Gateway drugs*. Detroit: Greenhaven Press.

Merino, N. (2011). *Drug legalization*. Farmington Hills, Mich: Greenhaven

    press.

Millard, B. (2013). *Legalization of Drugs: Conflict Theory*. Retrieved on May 31, 2014, from http://prezi.com/nlt7idyzaxwp/legalization-of-drugs-conflict-theory/

Morris, R. G., TenEyck, M., Barnes, J. C., & Kovandzic, T. V. (2014). The effect of medical marijuana laws on crime: evidence from state panel data, 1990-2006. PloS one, 9(3), e92816.

NIDA (2014). DrugFacts: *Marijuana*. Retrieved May 14, 2014, from http://www.drugabuse.gov/publications/drugfacts/marijuana

NIDA (2014). *Marijuana | NIDA for Teens*. Retrieved May, 14, 2014, from http://teens.drugabuse.gov/drug-facts/marijuana

Nunley, S., Alexander, B., Corns, R., & Geer, J. (2000). The Effects of Marijuana on Cognitive Functioning. Retrieved May 31, 2014, from http://www.unc.edu/~jdumas/projects/marijuana1.htm

Office of National Drug Control Policy (2008). TEEN MARIJUANA USE WORSENS DEPRESSION. Retrieved May 24, 2014, from https://www.ncjrs.gov/ondcppubs/publications/pdf/marij_mental_hlth.pdf

Oxford Dictionaries. (n.d.). Retrieved May 17, 2014 from http://www.oxforddictionaries.com/us

ProCon.org. (2012, December 31). How Many People in the United States Use Medical Marijuana? Retrieved on May 31, 2014, from http://medicalmarijuana.procon.org/view.answers.php?questionID=00 1199

Reingle, J. M., Staras, S. A., Jennings, W. G., Branchini, J., & Maldonado-Molina, M. M. (2012). The relationship between marijuana use and intimate partner violence in a nationally representative, longitudinal sample. Journal of interpersonal violence, 27(8), 1562-1578.

Roffman, R. A. (1982). *Marijuana as medicine.* Seattle: Madrona Publishers.

Saieva, A. P. (2008). *MARIJUANA LEGALIZATION: AMERICANS' ATTITUDES OVER FOUR DECADES* (Doctoral dissertation, University of Central Florida Orlando, Florida).

Shohov, T. (2003). *Medical use of marijuana: Policy, regulatory, and legal issues.* New York: Nova Science Publishers.

Shrivastava, A., Johnston, M., & Tsuang, M. (2011). *Cannabis use and cognitive dysfunction.* Indian journal of psychiatry, 53(3), 187.

Shukla, R. (2013). *Inside the Gate: Insiders' Perspectives on Marijuana as a Gateway Drug.*

Sidney, S., Beck, J. E., Tekawa, I. S., Quesenberry Jr., C. P., & Friedman, G.

    D. (1997). Marijuana Use and Mortality. *American Journal Of Public*

    Health, 87(4), 585-590

Swanson, C., Chamelin, N., Territo, L., & Taylor, R. (2009). *Criminal*

    Investigation (10th ed.). New York: McGraw-Hill.

Tardiff, J. C. (2008). *Marijuana*. Detroit: Greenhaven Press.

Tuyl, T. C. (2007). *Marijuana*. Detroit: Greenhaven Press.

Copyright © 2015 by Fuad A. Aljabri

All Rights Reserved

www.ingramcontent.com/pod-product-compliance
Lightning Source LLC
Chambersburg PA
CBHW081223170526
45165CB00009B/2930